Han and Juan Are Friends

by Meish Goldish
illustrated by Shelton Leong

Orlando   Boston   Dallas   Chicago   San Diego

Visit *The Learning Site!*

www.harcourtschool.com

Han likes to swim.
Juan likes to hike.

They both like to bike.
Han and Juan are friends!

Han likes chicken in rice.
Juan likes chicken in tortillas.

They both like to eat pizza.
Han and Juan are friends!

Han likes to play baseball.
Juan likes to play football.

They both like to play
basketball.
Han and Juan are friends!

Han likes a rainy day.
Juan likes a sunny day.

They both like a snowy day.
Han and Juan are friends!

Han likes to draw pictures.
Juan likes to write poems.

They both like to tell jokes.
Han and Juan are friends!

Han likes the park.
Juan likes the beach.

They both like to go to
school. Han and Juan are
friends!

Han and Juan are alike.
They are different, too.
Han and Juan can be
friends forever!